A Primer
On
Adult Children Of
Alcoholics

(Second Edition)

Timmen L. Cermak, MD

Health Communications, Inc.
Deerfield Beach, Florida

Timmen L. Cermak, MD
San Francisco, California

Library of Congress Cataloging-in-Publication Data

Cermak, Timmen L.
    A primer on adult children of alcoholics/Timmen L. Cermak. —
2nd ed.
        p.   cm.
    Bibliography: p.
    ISBN 1-55874-017-1
    1. Adult children of alcoholics.   2. Co-dependence (Psychol-
ogy)
    I. Title
HV5132.C44   1989   88-32262
362.2'92—dc19   CIP

Published by: Health Communications, Inc.
                    Enterprise Center
                    3201 S.W. 15th Street
                    Deerfield Beach, Florida 33442

Also by Timmen L. Cermak, MD

Diagnosing And Treating Co-dependence:
A Guide For Professionals

Evaluating And Treating
Adult Children Of Alcoholics:
A Guide for Professionals
(in press)

A Time To Heal

Contents

Preface To
The First Edition

I have written this booklet to provide adult children of alcoholics with information about themselves. I have not taken time to split hairs. All of the information may not apply to every reader. It may seem oversimplified, biased or simply wrong; however, most readers who accept these shortcomings will find much to stimulate and nurture them. This booklet comes from my experience as a psychiatrist and the director of an alcohol treatment unit, as well as direct treatment of Adult Children of Alcoholics and my own family experience. Its goal is to speak to the common bond among all adult children of alcoholics, uniting their minds, their hearts and their spirits.

1985

Preface To
The Second Edition

I first wrote the *Primer* as a handout for a workshop in Alaska. When I later heard that Xeroxed copies had made their way to friends and relatives as far away as Japan, I asked Health Communications if they would be interested in publishing it. Since then, over 45,000 copies have been sold, many to therapists who use it to introduce their clients to ACoA issues or as a stimulus for group discussions. The *Primer* has found a niche in the ACoA world. Its size is not imposing. Its language is simple and direct. And the majority of adult children of alcoholics are still awaiting their first introduction to the world of recovery.

In this second edition I have included new material, especially on recognizing emotional abuse, generalizing the ACoA experience to other dysfunctional families and turning a program of recovery into concrete changes in your life. I have also clarified points that confused earlier readers and answered the most frequent questions people have sent me.

The final motivation for writing this second edition came from my experience during a weekend visit to a friend's home in San Diego. His parents were there as well, and his father's life-long alcoholism was starting to take a greater toll. Each day the same cycle occurred. His father began the morning in an irritable mood. During the middle of the day he became pleasant, but by late afternoon he was isolating himself more and more. By dinnertime the sparks began to fly. Old hurts and angers were dredged up from the past and used as fuel for attacking whatever bothered him at the moment. The rest of the evening was spent progressively ignoring him.

The remarkable part of this experience is that I had a delightful time. It was a very pleasant visit. In part, my own recovery prevented me from focusing on the alcoholic's behavior. I was free to enjoy the rest of the people I was with. And, in part, my friend's family had learned over the years to disregard the father once he began getting intoxicated. By making him increasingly irrelevant, the family members protected themselves (and also quietly expressed their anger at him).

The end result is that **nothing** dramatic happened. There were no crises, no chaos or no horror stories to tell. I could easily imagine my friend telling a Twelve-Step meeting or a therapist, "I don't think my father's alcoholism had much of an effect. Nothing bad happened that I can remember." But I could see his pain and embarrassment were there, nonetheless.

Life with an alcoholic parent does not have to be dramatic to be painful. This point seems to be one of the most consistently misunderstood aspects of the ACoA experience. Many of the changes made throughout this second edition are geared toward helping you appreciate the fine and subtle ways in which "losing" your parent to alcohol, drugs or other problems can change the emotional atmosphere in which you live the rest of your life — until recovery begins.

1989

1

The Promise Of Hope For Adult Children Of Alcoholics

A s an adult child of an alcoholic (ACoA), there are good reasons for your being the kind of person you are.

Acknowledgment

The first step toward discovering these reasons is admitting that one or both of your parents are alcoholic. Such an acknowledgment often comes slowly. For many, it breaks family rules and the silence that deafens frightened families. It reveals secrets that have been hidden for years at great cost, and seems cold and hard, like a betrayal. It dredges up painful and sometimes ugly memories, and feels like picking at old wounds you have learned to live with quite well.

Denial

Thére are a host of good reasons for avoiding the fact that you are an adult child of an alcoholic. Your life is already sufficiently stressful; now is not a good time to add further strain. Or, your life is going well right now; why rock the boat unnecessarily? The good reasons are endless. The holidays are almost here; it's the day before my birthday or an exam; or it's Friday, Saturday or Sunday. . . . The truth is that all of these reasons are good; however, they are exactly the same reasons used by alcoholics to justify their decision not to look more realistically at their drinking.

Hope

The primary reason for taking inventory of how living with an alcoholic parent has affected you is the promise of hope. Because the compromises many ACoAs have made in their lives have seemed successful for so many years, they have faded out of their awareness and into the background. But each compromise quietly pulls in the reins on what can be hoped for in life. Eventually, ACoAs convince themselves that they are living full and rich lives, when actually they are settling for survival. This book is designed to show that you have a right to make choices in your life beyond mere survival. Does that sound too good to be true? Does that sound like a set-up to make you feel foolish for believing it? Perhaps you are already making choices in your life. Is it too much to hope that you can learn to make even more?

The promise is hope — hope to be freer than you have dared so far; hope to be healthier than you have imagined possible; and hope to feel more secure, more alive and more playful than you have ever felt.

This new hope must be nurtured. In order to grow, the hope needs constant exposure to the *truth* about your feelings, your memories, your fears, and the facts about your past and present life. For most of us, this new hope also needs constant exposure to other people — either those who are striving toward their own recovery or therapists with a specific interest in ACoAs. New hope is always fragile and does not flourish when it is hidden within the confines of our own minds. It needs the warmth of being shared with others.

The reward for exploring your feelings and what it means to be an adult child of an alcoholic is that you will begin allowing yourself to hope for a life that will become better than you have dared to dream. That hope is the harbinger of healing and comes like the first robin before the spring. It is yours for the price of acknowledging the realities of your life. That is the promise.

I cannot prove to you ahead of time that the promise will be kept. You will have to accept that on blind faith. But, whether you believe in the promise or not, it waits for you patiently. The promise is hope, and it's yours for the taking.

2

Resurrecting The Past

I s it necessary to resurrect the past, recalling old memories that have been laid to rest and old pains that you have worked to forget? No one can answer that question for you. For some ACoAs, the need to explore the effects of their parents' alcoholism is literally a matter of life and death. For others, it is less critical but can serve as a powerful avenue toward improving the quality of their lives. It has the potential for increasing the fullness and richness of experience that is available to them. Individuals must decide for themselves how "necessary" it is to look at what it means to be an ACoA.

Fears

Before you decide to resurrect the past, it may be helpful to look more closely at some attitudes that underlie any

reluctance you have. What is there to fear from a more in-
formed view of the past? A candid answer would be that *many*
fears are likely to arise: fear of abandonment, rage, betrayal
and sadness. Perhaps worst of all is fear of the unknown.
Don't minimize or ignore these fears; they are the
signposts you need to make progress on your journey. Be
aware that these fears can reach a magnitude great enough to
jeopardize your decision to continue moving forward. They
can hide for a time, and then surprise you by reemerging
when you least expect it. When they do reemerge, this is a
warning that the past is still very much alive and carries with
it some important unresolved issues.

You may feel that there is no sense in resurrecting a dead
past, or that life is simply too short to waste time on matters
seeming to be of no importance. However, our minds have
no fear of what is truly dead. Your fears are present because
the past is still present. You carry it around within yourself.

Freedom Is The Goal

Any feelings that are "resurrected" by this book are
feelings that continue living inside you today, whether or not
you are aware of them. Forgetting is not the goal, but
freedom is — freedom from the pain that comes from having
an alcoholic parent. What you forget, you are destined to
confront again and again. Freedom from pain comes through
allowing it to be as present and as deep as it truly is.

For some ACoAs, such freedom is necessary if they are to
continue growing or even to continue at all. For others, such
freedom will be a welcomed addition to an already
successful life. For most, an exploration of how their parents'
alcoholism continues to affect their present day life is an
excellent opportunity to learn how to experience deeper
levels of personal freedom. After all, it is difficult to imagine
any secret that is best kept in darkness, or any truth that does
not eventually lead to healing.

Avenue To Freedom

Although resurrecting the past often brings a lot of pain, do
not make the mistake of thinking that this pain is the goal.

Allowing yourself to experience this pain is simply the avenue we must all take to free ourselves of the past. When people get stuck in the pain, they may need professional help. Or they may need to recognize that they are not yet willing to have the pain.

Willing to have the pain? What could that mean?

It means that recovery comes through a willingness to acknowledge that you needed your parents, you probably loved your parents and alcohol prevented your parents from being fully attentive to you. Whenever we lose a parent prematurely, even if it is a partial loss, it hurts. If we resist that hurt, it goes underground and stays with us. We end up pretending our parents were less important than they really were. We separate ourselves a bit from reality. In coming back to what is real in our lives, we must be *willing* to feel the pain of that loss.

But, the pain is not the goal.

3

Who Is A Child Of An Alcoholic?

I t is estimated that 28 million Americans have at least one alcoholic parent. The enormity of such a number is hard to comprehend. Perhaps it is easier to think that one of every eight Americans is a child of an alcoholic (CoA). If all the CoAs stood shoulder-to-shoulder, the line would stretch from New York, to Seattle, to Los Angeles, to Atlanta, and back to New York. Although, as a CoA, you may have felt alone, you are a member of one of the largest groups in this country.

All Walks Of Life

These CoAs are your brothers and sisters. They come from all walks of life. Some are college graduates and have very successful careers, while many others are alcoholic or

addicted to other drugs. Some are in jail. The deep bond
between CoAs is forged out of sharing the common
experiences of fearing, loving, needing and hating the
alcoholic. The bond stems from having lived with an
alcoholic parent as the center of their lives. If you want to
experience the bond, look for it in the eyes of another ACoA
when you tell each other about your childhood. It is there in
the understanding with which your story is greeted.
Sometimes it is there in the way the other person's eyes have
trouble meeting yours without becoming overwhelmed by
the old pain. This is part of the common bond you share.

A lot of confusion comes from the large number of people
without alcoholic or drug-addicted parents who have
discovered that the ACoA characteristics (see Chapter 8)
describe their own lives. They have also discovered that
descriptions of what it *feels* like to be an ACoA match their
own experience. And the process of recovery applies as well.
Their identification with ACoA issues raises the question, "Can
a person be a 'CoA' without having an alcoholic parent?"

The crossover between adult children of alcoholics/drug
addicts and people from homes with other types of
dysfunction will be looked at in more detail in "Recognizing
Emotional Abuse" (Chapter 12). At this point it is enough to
say that the CoA field *has* begun to expand. What we have
learned about children of alcoholics is generally true for
children of other kinds of trauma as well. There are some
differences, but there is far more in common.

Historical Perspective

A little historical perspective might be helpful. A decade
ago very few people accepted that being a child of an
alcoholic was as dangerous to your health as being the child
of a schizophrenic or being sexually abused, for example.
Today the tables are turned. Adult children of schizophrenics
and survivors of sexual abuse are asking to be included in
workshops for ACoAs. The speed with which the trauma of
being the child of an alcoholic has been accepted into the
mainstream of our country's awareness is breathtaking.

The inclusion of many varieties of trauma into the CoA movement makes perfect sense. It confirms that the CoA experience is genuinely traumatic. And it brings the process of recovery, which developed within the alcoholism world, to a wider and equally needy population.

But, for the individual ACoA — for you — it still remains important to look in detail at your own *specific* reality: life with an alcoholic parent.

4

What Is Alcoholism?

Many ACoAs find themselves caught in an internal debate about whether or not their parent is really an alcoholic. This is a normal stage in the denial process. Just as people who have a terminal illness try to find relief from the truth by simply not believing it, ACoAs find it hard to admit their parent is an alcoholic. At other times, such questioning stems from ignorance. Perhaps the reality of their parent's drinking has been shielded from the child's view by the nonalcoholic parent, out of caring or embarrassment. Sometimes there is simply a lack of information about the disease we call "alcoholism."

When Galileo asked the priests to look through his telescope at the heavenly bodies, they refused. They were certain the telescope would be playing tricks on them if it

showed them anything other than what they expected. Just
for a few moments, put your preconceived notions on the
back burner and try to look at the "disease concept of
alcoholism" as Galileo's telescope. Go ahead; give it a try.
Look through it at your parent this way, and you will see that
the disease of alcoholism has many aspects, some of which
extend beyond the alcoholic. Alcoholism is simultaneously a
physical, mental, family and spiritual disease.

Alcoholism As A Physical Disease

To begin with, alcoholism is a physical disease. Not
everyone who drinks equal amounts of alcohol becomes
addicted. Some people experience blackouts (memory
failures) the first time they become intoxicated. Male
children of alcoholic fathers become alcoholic at four to nine
times the normal rate of the general population. This occurs
even if they are adopted by a nonalcoholic couple at birth.
On one level, alcoholism is a physical disease like diabetes.
However, unlike diabetes, once it becomes active, its major
impact is to affect the one organ most needed to regain
health — the brain.

Alcoholism As A Mental Disease

On another level, alcoholism is a mental disease. Once
people are physically addicted to alcohol, even to a minor
degree, their mental functions are altered. They can no
longer feel emotions keenly nor can they think with
maximum clarity. One champion motorcycle driver discovered that he was unable to regain his peak lap times for over
two weeks after a one-night binge.

Alcoholism is a mental disease because the chronic use of
alcohol (or any other drug that is specifically ingested in
order to alter brain function and thus to alter experience)
diminishes the capacity for self-observation, complete
honesty and psychological growth. Alcoholics' abilities to
assess their lives and the actual sources of their misery is
compromised by the very disease they must come to terms
with in order to regain health. Brains that are chronically, or

even intermittently, bathed in toxic substances cannot support the complex, sophisticated and mature psychological processes needed for healing. Gradually, alcoholics learn to deal with the world from a position of defense, using denial, blaming and rationalization. They see the cause of their misery as lying outside themselves. Drinking is seen more as a reaction to that misery than as the cause. When alcoholics stop drinking, it often becomes painfully apparent that their denial and blaming do not stop. They continue as ingrained habits. Recovery is a long process of recognizing these defensive attitudes and gradually relinquishing them.

Alcoholism As A Family Disease

Alcoholism is also a family disease. The idea that the family unit can be diseased is, at first, difficult to understand and accept. It simply means that good people can hurt each other when they try to conform to the distorted rules that govern alcoholic families. They can also find themselves living in a virtual ᵗate of isolation. It is nearly impossible for people to live with an active alcoholic for any substantial period of time and maintain an objective perspective. Instead, family members almost invariably begin to feel embarrassed by the alcoholic's behavior, guilty about not doing enough and responsible for trying to get the alcoholic to stop drinking. Sometimes the family members make excuses for the drinking or deny that it is harmful, trying to do the best they can while wearing the blinders of denial.

Alcoholism As A Spiritual Disease

Alcoholism *is* a spiritual disease, which is not the same as a sin. At the deepest levels, alcoholics have fallen into a distorted relationship with themselves and with the universe as a whole. Balanced between the forces of life and death, alcoholics seem incapable of the spiritual clarity required for a commitment to either.

Certainly it can be seen that an intoxicated brain is not likely to have the delicate sensitivity for meditating on the subtle bonds that connect us all to each other and to the universe at large. If a Higher Power is speaking to us, it is most likely in a whisper. We need all our faculties to catch even a small portion of what there is to learn. At a minimum, spirituality is the word used to indicate the whole range of relationships that define who we are: the relationship of our present consciousness to our underlying sense of identity, and our relationship to others, to life, to the planet as a whole, to the universe and to our Higher Power. The next chapter explains how excessive drinking is just one manifestation of the distorted relationships that trouble the lives of alcoholics and those around them.

5

What Is Co-dependence?

The following common scenario demonstrates the distorted relationships that exist in an alcoholic family and the part that all family members play in maintaining these distortions.

A couple sits in my office with their backs turned slightly toward each other. Their eldest child, near tears, is seated between them. Both parents are ready to explode with anger that is hidden beneath stony expressions. They don't talk openly about what is going on between them. Both parents deny feeling anything. The child appears afraid to cry and claims things are better now that the drinking has stopped. One parent looks at the child with disgust. The other looks on with pity and reaches out to hold the child's hand, but the child pulls away.

Who is the alcoholic in the family? It could be any one of the three. Does it matter? Something about the behavior of these three people is similar. That something is called co-dependence.

Co-dependence should be distinguished from interdependence. When two people (or two nations) become interdependent, both give the other power over their welfare. On the other hand, when two people become co-dependent, both give the other power over their self-esteem. When someone fails you in an interdependent relationship, you suffer from a loss of money, time, etc. But, when someone fails you in a co-dependent relationship, you suffer a loss of *self-esteem.*

Co-dependents live according to a set of unspoken rules, which validate and legitimize the belief that their sense of self-worth stems from how those close to them behave. In order to feel good about themselves, they direct their energy toward making others happy. They flatter themselves by saying they are loving, caring for and saving another person. The truth is they are trying to control other people's lives in an effort to make their own lives more secure. In the process, they give others a great deal of power over themselves.

When we are in a co-dependent relationship with someone who is doing well, it is hard to imagine that the relationship is anything but a healthy alliance. This kind of situation permits two people, who are unable to feel good within themselves, to capture a sense of self-acceptance through their connection to each other. The cost of building one's self-worth in this way increases as time goes on. The ties between co-dependents become constraints. Soon both partners feel imprisoned by their inability to tolerate rejection and exhausted by the burden of responsibility for the other's security and happiness. Their intolerance of rejection literally locks them in the co-dependent relationship.

As both members of a co-dependent relationship become increasingly stressed, one member usually can no longer continue the role and seeks some kind of relief. This person often finds that alcohol eases the tensions of the co-dependent lifestyle, making it more tolerable and thus enabling its continuation. According to this view of co-dependence, it is clear that all alcoholics are co-dependent and that the co-dependence often precedes the alcoholism.

Once active alcoholism is established, the nonalcoholic's co-dependence also tends to take a turn for the worse. The nonalcoholic is unable to live with or without the alcoholic. In an effort to regain some control over their lives, nonalcoholics try to beg, barter or cajole alcoholics to stop drinking. Their goal is to have a return to the earlier co-dependent relationship that had the appearance of working well.

Five Characteristics Of Co-dependence

In a book for therapists (*Diagnosing And Treating Co-dependence,* Johnson Institute Books, 1986) I have offered a detailed description of co-dependent behavior. This can all be condensed into five characteristics. As you read through these characteristics, you can look at yourself for evidence of your own co-dependence.

First Characteristic

Co-dependents change who they are and what they are feeling to please others.

Co-dependents are split between two worlds. One world is the facade that we show other people — the false version of ourselves. The other world is how chaotic, fearful and empty our life feels underneath. Co-dependents put on a front while they are crying or dying inside. They do this to protect themselves from the fear that things will only get worse if they let people know how they really feel, or who they really are.

When we are co-dependent, we sacrifice our own identities in order to feel close to others. We change who we are in order to please other people. And, in the process, who we really are becomes more and more of a stranger even to ourselves. Ultimately, co-dependents no longer know who they are or what they want, unless they are in a relationship and can take their cues from another person.

Second Characteristic

Co-dependents feel responsible for meeting other people's needs, even at the expense of their own needs.

Co-dependents have their antennae up and working all the time, scouting the environment, watching people's faces and listening to their tone of voice, always searching for signs of their disapproval or looking for ways to fix *their* problems. We actually get more upset if others are disappointed or hurt than if our *own* problems go unsolved.

Most of us co-dependents believe we act like this because we are so generous. But real generosity stems from love that seeks no return. The truth is that co-dependents are so afraid of rejection that they will do anything to keep other people happy, including sacrificing their own needs in order to keep people from leaving them.

How many of you feel like you have been pulled in a hundred directions by other people's demands and needs, and wish you could have just ten minutes at the end of a day to do what *you* want to? How many of us do not know how to say no when we should?

Third Characteristic

Co-dependents have low self-esteem.

Most chemically dependent people feel ashamed of themselves. Despite their defensiveness and anger toward others, most are inwardly very critical of themselves. So perhaps it isn't strange that family members also begin to feel bad about themselves.

For co-dependents, low self-esteem comes from two main places:

• It comes from having very little *sense* of self to esteem. By always pleasing others and by always giving our power away, we turn our whole identity over to them until we don't even know who we are any more. It's hard to respect people who seem afraid to exist, even when it's yourself!

- Low self-esteem also comes from believing that we truly *are* responsible for someone else's disease or alcohol/drug use. Once we believe this, we will always feel inadequate when we can't control the chemical dependent's behavior. This mistaken sense of what *should* be under our control is at the very core of both co-dependence and chemical dependence. (We'll look at it further in a moment.)

Once low self-esteem is accepted as what we deserve to feel, it reinforces our belief that we need to please other people because we have no faith that anyone would tolerate being with us unless we are serving them. As you can see, each of the characteristics of co-dependence reinforces the others until a web of beliefs and behavior takes over your life.

Fourth Characteristic

Co-dependents are driven by compulsions.

Most of us know what it's like to feel that our life is being *driven* and that we do not have any real choices about what is happening to us. Co-dependents typically feel compelled to keep the family together, to stop the drinking or other drug use, to save the family from shame, to work, to eat or diet, to take physical risks, to spend or gamble, to have affairs, to be religious, to keep the house clean and on and on. . . .

The driven quality that compulsions bring into your life accomplishes two things:

- First, it creates excitement and drama. As we battle our compulsions, the adrenalin begins to flow, and simple decisions, such as what to eat or how much to work, are turned into life and death struggles. This drama temporarily gives a feeling of being more fully alive.
- Second, compulsions occupy a lot of time and block us from our deeper feelings. Co-dependents often get locked into compulsive behaviors to avoid more painful feelings of fear, sadness, anger and abandonment caused by someone's chemical dependence.

Fifth Characteristic

Co-dependents have the same use of denial and distorted relationship to willpower that is typical of active alcoholics and other drug addicts.

This brings us to the core of co-dependence. During your recovery, developing a more realistic relationship with willpower is the eye of the needle through which we all *must* pass if we are ever going to find the freedom, joy and self-esteem we long for.

When Vernon Johnson wrote *I'll Quit Tomorrow*, he described the "ism" of alcoholism as being precisely the same symptoms we see in other family members. By the "ism" of alcoholism, we mean the way of life that alcoholics fall into as a result of their drinking.

Denial and an unwillingness to accept human limitations are the two most destructive parts of the "ism" of alcoholism. In their own way, co-dependent family members fall into the same distorted relationship to reality and willpower. Just like the alcoholic, we deny reality and think we can change anything if we use enough willpower. Let's look at some of the parallels.

Chemically dependent people deny that they are abusing alcohol and other drugs. They refuse to see how their alcohol/drug use is ruining their lives and their relationships with family members, friends and even some co-workers.

Co-dependents show exactly the same denial. They often refuse to see that a family member is chemically dependent or they refuse to acknowledge that their children are being hurt. Shame and compulsion to keep things under control cause co-dependents to underestimate the problem. They hide the problem from others who might be able to help. They hide their feelings from themselves. And they deny their own compulsive behavior. . . . Denial is a universal human trait, but it is overused by *every* member of a chemically dependent family. Your very refusal to see this may be one more way that your denial is at work.

Co-dependents are driven by the firm belief that their coping strategies fail because of personal inadequacy. When we can't control the drinking or other drug use of someone we love, we blame ourselves for not trying hard enough or for not trying the right way. There's nothing wrong with trying to figure out how to help someone who is chemically dependent, as long as we realize that we are not the cause of it and that we can not control or cure it. But, when our own overbearing sense of responsibility and self-esteem begin blinding us to the fact that we do not have direct power to stop another person's chemical dependence, we actually become part of the problem.

When co-dependents take too much responsibility for other persons' recovery, it keeps the chemical dependents from having to see the reality of their disease. *No* one is to blame and *no* one has the power to control chemical dependence. Once the disease is present, no one can will it away.

The ability of our willpower to change the world is far more limited than most of us want to believe. We co-dependents are stubborn about looking realistically at the limits of our willpower, especially the limits of our willpower to control other people or our own emotions.

The Bottom Line About Co-dependence

The five characteristics of co-dependence presented here can help you identify any tendency in yourself to be a co-dependent. Above all, co-dependence is an internal feeling. Like alcoholism, it makes little difference if someone else is putting the label on you. What matters is whether you feel that the label fits yourself. Perhaps the definition of a co-dependent is best expressed by the saying, "when co-dependents die, it's someone else's life that passes before their eyes."

---

*This chapter on co-dependence borrows heavily from the videotape *"Co-dependence: The Joy Of Recovery,"* featuring Timmen L. Cermak. The tape is available through Johnson Institute, 1-(800) 231-5165.

6

Can Co-dependence Be Overcome?

T here is a distorted attitude about willpower that pervades all co-dependent thinking, feeling and behavior. At the core of co-dependency is an overwhelming devotion to willpower. The idea of being able to overcome life's problems by sheer force of will is the central delusion. Co-dependence cannot be overcome, and only a co-dependent would persist in such an effort.

Paradoxical Nature Of Willpower

The paradoxical nature of willpower has been recognized in the field of alcoholism treatment, at least since the birth of Alcoholics Anonymous (AA) in 1935. Since all alcoholics are also co-dependent, it should be expected that recovery from both hinges on individuals' willingness to reassess their relationship to willpower. Perhaps a parable would be useful here:

A youngster was beaten by a huge bully several years his senior while walking home from school. Out of embarrass-ment, he made a deal with his friends that he would never let this happen again. The next day he ran an errand on the way home that took him a different route. When he was asked if he beat the bully that day, the boy explained that they had not met, but if they had, he would have made the bully pay dearly. The next day he stayed late at school, and the bully was nowhere to be seen when he ran home. This time his friends began to doubt that the boy could defeat the bully. They thought, perhaps, he was really more afraid than he admitted. The boy was determined that he would lick the bully or else. As the year went by and the boy continued to avoid meeting the bully, even he began to feel weak-willed. Eventually, he forced himself to challenge the bully in order to regain his self-esteem and was again soundly beaten.

Evidently, as demonstrated by the experience of the young boy in this story, willpower cannot change every reality. We have limited power to determine those things over which we have control and those over which we have no control. Clearly, alcoholics are involved in trying to use willpower to change how their bodies react to alcohol, thereby denying the existence of their illness. Diabetics might just as well try to exert willpower to control their blood sugar level, or you and I try to use willpower to counter the force of gravity after stepping off a cliff.

The universe decides what we, as humans, have under our potential control. Much, but not all, of our behavior is subject to our will, while the behavior of others is not. Our will has a great deal of power over our attention and over what we choose to attach it to. We are free to limit conscious awareness of our feelings, but we have little power over whether or not we have feelings, or what those feelings will be.

Co-dependents act as though they have the power to bring all manner of things under their control, simply by their willing it to be so. Despite the accumulation of overwhelming evidence that this attitude is self-destructive, they press on with it. Nonalcoholic co-dependents believe they can get others to stop drinking by saying or doing just the right thing. They also believe that they can put aside their anger, and in so doing the anger will cease to exist. Every time their willpower fails to achieve its goal, their self-esteem falls (as was true for the boy in the parable). The typical response of co-dependents to such failure is to redouble their efforts to make the impossible happen.

The co-dependent's efforts are all so noble. There is a song from the musical *Don Quixote* entitled "The Impossible Dream," which could be the co-dependent's anthem. Willpower is revered, even worshipped, as the most laudable avenue toward self-esteem. Alcoholics repeatedly demonstrate an inability to control the effect of alcohol on their bodies and then seek solace in the fact that at least they are locked in mortal combat with their problems. Willpower contains the seeds of its own destruction when it begins to exceed the boundaries of what is possible. Alcoholics who try to defeat alcoholism by avoiding alcohol will eventually feel like the boy who is still avoiding the bully. Then it becomes a matter of self-esteem to test oneself, usually by taking just one drink. The alcoholic uses willpower again and again to master the impossible, and the failure to do so is interpreted as a sign that one's willpower is still not quite strong enough.

Freedom From Co-dependence

The first step in recovery for any alcoholic is nicely stated by AA: "We admitted that we are powerless over alcohol — that our lives had become unmanageable." This admission strikes directly at the heart of one's co-dependence and must be made in one form or another by every co-dependent interested in recovery. Our powers are limited. We are not God. And the limits of our power are frequently dictated to us by the world at large. We are powerless to determine what shall be in our power and what shall not. We are so very far from being omnipotent that it is frightening. Our lives cannot run smoothly by conscious control, which we use like a traffic cop trying to bring order out of a Mardi Gras crowd. Once the clowns and kings are put in line and once the feelings and impulses are brought under "proper" control, it is no longer a Mardi Gras crowd. It is no longer life. Life cannot be managed because it is far too rich, too spontaneous and too rambunctious to be fully understood by our thinking, controlling minds.

Co-dependence cannot be overcome. All efforts to conquer it only add fuel to an already raging fire. But, we can free ourselves from being captive to our co-dependent patterns, just as alcoholics can free themselves from being slaves to their disease. This freedom comes only when we are willing to trust that our lives will turn out better when they are no longer managed, controlled or constantly bullied by our willpower.

7

Co-dependent Family Roles

On the surface, co-dependent families may differ from each other, but they have a great deal in common beneath that surface. When a co-dependent becomes chemically dependent as well, the family system takes on a more rigid structure, with all the other members limiting themselves by the specific roles they play to support the system. For example, co-dependent spouses may resort to the use of chemicals as well, or perhaps deny that any problems exist, remaining unaware that their partner is an alcoholic. Alternatively, they may play a martyr role and devote their lives to an effort to rescue the alcoholic. Another role that is often assumed by the spouse is that of a prosecutor devoted to punishing or shaming the alcoholic into sobriety. The truth is that most spouses fall into one or the other of these categories. Spouses who are not co-dependent do not allow their own self-destruction to proceed in step with the alcoholic's decline. The alcoholic either gets into treatment, or the marriage tends to unravel.

In a similar manner, children in a co-dependent/alcoholic family discover that the number of roles available to them are limited. The advantage of playing one or another of these roles is simply that it buys them a place at the family table. Of course, co-dependents delude themselves into believing that these roles have no price. But they do have a price, and it is often quite dear. The price is your own individuality.

Primary Family Roles

Sharon Wegscheider (in *Another Chance*) identifies the primary family roles for children as the hero, the scapegoat, the lost child and the mascot. In the midst of alcoholic chaos, heroes attempt to hold things together, to mediate and to make up for their parents' deficiencies. The scapegoats misbehave in ways that will attract attention and give people something on which to focus besides alcoholism. The lost children fade into the woodwork and become masters at avoiding blame and being caught in the middle. Mascots simply become irrelevant distracters; they clown about or create enough diversion so that no one's attention stays focused on one's problems too long.

Adult children of alcoholics frequently recognize these roles as those played out in their own families. The best way to identify the role you adopt is to look at your predominate feelings whenever family life becomes chaotic. Heroes tend to feel inadequate and guilty, while scapegoats feel hurt and angry. Lost children feel lonely, and mascots feel fear. As you recall what happened in your family when you were a child, notice the feelings that accompany the memories. These feelings will be your best clue to the role you most often played. Once you have identified your role, try feeling the price you paid for taking that role.

Roles Determined By Family Need

When ACoAs identify strongly with one or more of these roles, it often helps them see for the first time how their behavior was dictated more by the *family's* needs than by their own inherent personality. This is the real violence done by alcoholic family roles. The roles themselves are not the problem. People in healthy families also sort themselves out into different roles. But, in healthy families, people develop their role from their own individual talents and needs. These roles also remain more flexible. In alcoholic families, on the other hand, the roles tend to be rigidly imposed on you. Your role is handed to you; you are expected to play that role, whether it fits your personality or not, whenever the family is in trouble.

8

Characteristics
Of ACoAs

The list of ACoA characteristics is long and wide-ranging. No single person could possibly exhibit all of these characteristics. As you browse through them, it is entirely up to you to try each one on to determine how well it fits. Many non-ACoAs may find the following descriptions also fit them. This should not be surprising. The trauma of living with emotionally absent and co-dependent parents can occur in many ways; an alcoholic family is only one form the problem can take. The bottom line is this: If you feel your life is described by many of the characteristics listed below, and one of your parents is alcoholic, then you should know that a blueprint exists for recovering your sense of freedom and dignity. (See Chapters 13-17.)

These characteristics should be read as descriptions and not as indictments. Initially, you may see them as deficits and

33

liabilities. However, during recovery you will learn that they can become assets, once you develop the freedom to use them appropriately.

The Characteristics Of ACoAs*

Fear Of Losing Control

Adult children of alcoholics maintain control of their feelings and behavior, and try to control the feelings and behavior of others. They do not do this to hurt either themselves or others, but out of fear. They fear their lives will get worse if they let go of their control and get uncomfortably anxious when control is not possible.

Fear Of Feelings

Adult children of alcoholics have buried their feelings (especially anger and sadness) from childhood on and have lost the ability to feel or express emotions freely. Eventually, all intense feelings are feared, even good feelings, such as joy and happiness.

Fear Of Conflict

Adult children of alcoholics are frightened by people in authority, angry people and personal criticism. Common assertiveness displayed by others is often misinterpreted as anger. As a result of their fear of conflict, ACoAs are constantly seeking approval, but they lose their identity in the process. They often end up in a self-imposed state of isolation.

Overdeveloped Sense Of Responsibility

Adult children of alcoholics are hypersensitive to the needs of others. Their self-esteem comes from how others view them, and thus they have a compulsive need to be perfect.

Feelings Of Guilt

When ACoAs stand up for themselves instead of giving in to others, they feel guilty. ACoAs sacrifice their own needs in an effort to be "responsible" and to avoid guilt.

Inability To Relax, Let Go And Have Fun

Fun is stressful for ACoAs, especially when others are watching. The child inside is terrified, exercising all the control it can muster to be good enough just to survive. Under such rigid control, it's no wonder spontaneity suffers, for spontaneity and control are incompatible.

Harsh, Even Fierce, Self-Criticism

Adult children of alcoholics are burdened by a very low sense of self-esteem, no matter how competent they may be in many areas.

Living In A World Of Denial

Whenever ACoAs feel threatened, their tendency toward denial intensifies.

Difficulties With Intimate Relationships

Intimacy gives ACoAs a feeling of being out of control. It requires self-love and comfort with expressing one's own needs. As a result, ACoAs frequently have difficulty with sexuality. They repeat relationship patterns without growth.

Living Life From The Viewpoint Of A Victim

Adult children of alcoholics may be either aggressive or passive victims, and they are often attracted to other "victims" in their love, friendship and career relationships.

Compulsive Behavior

Adult children of alcoholics may work compulsively, eat compulsively, become addicted to a relationship or behave in other compulsive ways. Most tragically, ACoAs may drink compulsively and become alcoholics themselves.

Tendency To Confuse Love And Pity

As a result of this confusion, ACoAs often "love" people they can pity and rescue.

Fear Of Abandonment

Adult children of alcoholics will do anything to hold onto a relationship in order not to experience the pain of abandonment.

Tendency To Assume A Black And White Perspective Under Pressure

The gray areas of life disappear, and ACoAs see themselves facing an endless series of either/or alternatives.

Tendency Toward Physical Complaints

Adult children of alcoholics suffer higher rates of stress-related medical illnesses.

Suffering From Backlog Of Delayed Grief

Losses experienced during childhood were often never grieved for because the alcoholic family does not tolerate such intensely uncomfortable feelings. Current losses cannot be felt without calling up these past feelings. As a result, ACoAs are frequently depressed.

Tendency To React Rather Than To Act

Adult children of alcoholics remain hypervigilant, constantly scanning the environment for potential catastrophes.

Ability To Survive

If you are reading this booklet, you are a survivor.

Rules That Govern Alcoholic Families

Claudia Black, in her book *It Will Never Happen To Me*, summarizes these characteristics in her set of three rules that govern alcoholic families:

> **Don't Talk.**
> **Don't Trust.**
> **Don't Feel.**

Children of alcoholics learn at a very young age that their emotional, and even physical, survival depends on learning and following these rules. That was a reality. They were not imagining things.

As adults, they often fail to recognize that these rules are no longer necessary outside the alcoholic family. Instead, they rarely speak from the wellspring of simple truths within. They don't do anything as foolish or vulnerable as to trust, to really trust other people, and they blindly maintain a tight rein on their feelings. The rules that once were the means of survival have become a noose that is slowly and inextricably squeezing the life out of them.

---

*Both the "Problems and Solutions" (anonymous), and Jane Middelton (workshop presentations), were relied on in compiling the list of ACoA characteristics. The author acknowledges his appreciation for these resources.

=9=

Understanding ACoA Characteristics

Many ACoA characteristics obviously stem from the co-dependent style of coping with problems that children are taught in alcoholic families. But this is not the whole story. Adult children of alcoholics not only suffer from ineffective ways of dealing with life's stresses but also suffer from the sheer level of stress that wove in and out of their daily lives. Many of the characteristics in the previous chapter are related mostly to this traumatic stress.

Post-Traumatic Stress Disorder

The phenomenon of Post-Traumatic Stress Disorder (PTSD), which is linked in most people's minds to the difficulties some Vietnam veterans have had in readjusting to civilian life, is a helpful model for understanding many of the characteristics seen in ACoAs. When people are subject to stresses of such intensity and nature that they clearly lie outside the range of normal human experience, PTSD occurs. The effects are especially severe if the stress is caused by a *series* of traumatic events and is of human origin. The effects are even more severe if the individual under stress has rigid coping strategies or if the person's support system includes those who encourage denial of the stress.

It is essential for ACoAs and for those interested in understanding them to acknowledge that growing up with an alcoholic parent is not normal. Early childhood development within an alcoholic family system constitutes a stress that is clearly outside the range of human experience usually considered to be normal. If this statement is not accepted, then one is left believing that parental alcoholism is a normal state of affairs. God help us if we ever get to the point of believing that.

An alcoholic family stresses a child well beyond such normal events as the birth of a sibling, beginning school or even the death of a parent. Alcoholic families generate a daily environment of inconsistency, chaos, fear, abandonment, denial, symbolic death, and real or potential violence. Such a prolonged series of stresses, so clearly of human origin, would be expected to evoke significant symptoms of distress in most individuals. The symptoms of PTSD are similar enough to the characteristics of ACoAs to suggest that growing up in an alcoholic family leaves people suffering from elements of PTSD.

Imagine, for a moment, being eighteen years old and suddenly lost in the jungles of Vietnam, listening to your platoon leader's gasping breath after a piece of shrapnel has severed his windpipe. Then imagine you are four years old and are spending the day at home with your mother. It is early morning and she is hung over and sick. She screams at you to get your own breakfast and stays in bed until ten o'clock. After an eye opener, she asks you what you want for lunch. After a couple more drinks, she is fully alive again. Lunch is a time of playfulness and companionship with her.

The two of you plan to go to the store to get an ice cream cone. Two hours and too many drinks later, she is beginning to get surly and shouts at you to quiet down. Now, it's four o'clock and you find her motionless on the living room floor. You bend down to hear if she is still breathing. You're scared and wish Daddy would come home soon and keep Mommy alive. Finally, your father arrives home; he is angry but never says anything about Mommy lying on the floor. You follow him around the kitchen in silence, trying to act grown-up and in control by helping with dinner.

Symptoms Of Post-Traumatic Stress Disorder

The powerful images above cry out to be taken seriously. They describe realities experienced by millions of Americans, whose lives were changed by such extreme events. People with PTSD experience the original trauma over and over again. They may report becoming obsessed with recurrent, intrusive thoughts, images and feelings. They may experience nightmares or the sudden reemergence of whole patterns of behavior and feelings associated with the original trauma when confronted with its symbolic equivalent, such as a fire cracker being reacted to as if it were a rifle shot. In a similar way, ACoAs are obsessive about their guilt and responsibilities, even to a family that they have left across the country, or whose members have long been dead. (Adult children of alcoholics know that alcoholic parents never die, they just lie under the ground in waiting.) What ACoA has not experienced a sudden surge of defensiveness, fear or guilt when confronting a boss or facing a traffic policeman? These feelings seem to be only an instant away from the feelings they had as children, which is a major reason they take such constant care to keep them under control.

Post-Traumatic Stress Disorder also leads to a condition called psychic numbing. This is experienced as a sense of estrangement and disconnection, to the point of feeling there is no place or group to which we belong. Psychic numbing, at its worst, leads to dissociative states, which involve a phasing out into the ultimate denial of what is currently happening. Emotions become constricted, especially in the areas where intimacy, tenderness and sexuality are involved. This lack of spontaneity and extreme control of emotions is a hallmark of people who have suffered severe trauma (such as physical or sexual abuse). Many ACoAs speak of how they are able to tolerate extremely miserable situations by maintaining a facade of being present and attentive, while quietly retreating to very distant and safer places in their imagination. Such denial eventually becomes indistinguishable from dissociation, which is a temporary inability to identify with one's immediate realities.

Symptoms of PTSD also include hyperalertness, excessive nervous activity and generalized anxiety. Unexpected sounds often startle people with PTSD, and many Vietnam veterans suffer from survivor guilt, which leads to chronic depressive symptoms. People with PTSD unconsciously mold their entire lives to avoid any activities that recall the original trauma. Again, the parallel to ACoAs is obvious.

How does an ACoA's co-dependence interact with what has just been said about PTSD? It is here that the family's belief in willpower becomes most self-destructive. Co-dependents are particularly subject to the effects of PTSD. Since co-dependents are very practiced at using denial, they ignore the chronic stress they feel and minimize its effects. Over-reliance on willpower pushes co-dependents beyond their tolerance level for stress. Their tendency to deny the existence of stress simply leads to the absorption of even more stress and intensifies the resulting emotional constriction. In the end, co-dependents see each effect of the chronic stress as a symptom of their own inadequacy, and their self-esteem falls even further. It should be no surprise that, during the recovery process, ACoAs frequently experience plummeting self-esteem when they take that first realistic look at how deeply and pervasively they have been affected by growing up in an alcoholic home.

The characteristics of ACoAs are best seen as a combination of co-dependence and Post-Traumatic Stress Disorder. ACoAs are *not* guilty of excessive or distorted reactions to normal events. Instead, they are left with the remnants of essentially normal reactions to abnormal events. The process of recovery involves a shift from seeing yourself as abnormal, to seeing the experience of growing in an alcoholic home as abnormal.

—10—

How Do ACoA Characteristics Develop During Childhood?

Childhood is the foundation upon which the rest of our lives is built, just as concrete blocks and cement provide a foundation for a building. This foundation must be laid in a series of stages if it is to be strong. The first stage involves having a physical and emotional environment that can be trusted. In the second stage, the sense of oneself as a separate individual develops. The third stage is the stage in which children develop initiative and a sense of mastery. The trials, errors and success achieved in this stage provide solid cornerstones for further growth. The fourth stage prepares children for the final separation from parents that eventually must take place in order to create a family of one's own.

Each of these stages rests upon the successful completion of all the preceding stages. If the childhood foundation is to

stand with integrity and longevity, the tasks belonging to
each stage must be completed in their proper sequence.

Stage One — Basic Trust

During the first year of life, we develop our basic sense of
whether the world is an inviting and supportive place for us,
or whether it is a hostile environment. A basic sense of trust
is largely dependent on our parents' ability to respond to our
needs with consistency and accuracy. It is important that
parents focus their attention according to the infant's
schedule more than their own. A mutual regulation process
needs to occur between infants and their parents, in order for
children to develop confidence in themselves and others.

Alcoholic families are often too obsessed with alcohol and
the alcoholic to provide the *focused attention*, consistently
adequate care and mutual regulation that children need to
build a basic trust in themselves and the world around them.
Instead, these children learn to adapt their needs as much as
possible to the random availability of care. Consequently,
they may develop a tendency to withdraw from people.
During the first year of life, children in this kind of
environment often begin converting efforts to communicate
with and control the environment into a precocious over-
control of themselves. What has happened? The basic site of
the foundation on which the personality is to be built is
untrustworthy. It feels as though it is being constructed on an
unstable earthquake fault.

Stage Two — Autonomy

The next stage of building the foundation involves
exerting control over the environment. This stage is
represented by the impulse toward autonomy and the
exercising of self-control displayed by two-year-olds. Here is
where we end our absolute dependence on our parents, and
begin the process of balancing closeness and distance:
holding on and letting go. Successfully developing a sense of
autonomy is easiest, first, if we have developed a basic trust,
and then if our parents understand and encourage the

changes our growth produces in the family. Children of alcoholics can be hindered at this second stage because their chemically dependent parent is struggling on a daily basis with similar problems of impulse control and autonomy. As a result, there is rarely the consistent discipline, as well as flexible, loving, external control needed to facilitate the child's first efforts to differentiate from the parents. Children at this stage are nearly defenseless against the projection of blame that is so rampant in co-dependent families. Consequently, these children begin to demonstrate an overdeveloped sense of responsibility for others. They begin to experience feelings of shame and self-doubt when they see their actions as a cause of their parents' drinking. To combat these feelings, they frequently develop a desperate need to please and a compulsion to be perfect.

Stage Three — Initiative And Mastery

The ability of children to work toward their *own* goals determines the ultimate integrity of their adult life. Children, who have successfully come to trust the world and to see themselves as separate people, can then enter into a stage of developing their initiative and a sense of mastery. They begin playing in a way that incorporates practice until they have climbed the biggest tree in the yard. They enjoy success for its own sake.

It is at this point (age four-six) that alcoholic families often expect a child to become too self-sufficient. The task that began as play quickly becomes a chore, and children feel compelled to be responsible for themselves in order to avoid being a burden to the family. The need to be competent is driven by necessity and anxiety, not by pleasure. Children become little adults and often take pride in their own precociousness, unaware that the price for aborting childhood will be paid later in life, and the cost will be significant.

Is it any surprise that children of alcoholics identify primarily with their alcoholic parent? Even those who have become pseudoadults feel a sense of helplessness, failure and lack of control within. Although they appear mature and capable, they have failed to develop a sense of themselves as separate and sovereign individuals. Their path of development has led them to a blind alley. Just as alcoholics find refuge from their feelings when intoxicated but never obtain real security through drinking, ACoAs develop successful survival skills. However, they never gain access to either the spontaneity of youth or the richness and security of full maturity. They obtain an illusion of their goal of safety but at a price of being even further from real security.

Stage Four — Separation

Once the foundation is secure, attention is turned toward separation from family. Children must stop focusing primarily on their families of origin if they ever hope to separate enough to begin their *own* families. Even for the healthiest of families, this is frequently a difficult and painful time, but alcoholic families simply do not permit or accept separation. ACoAs experience feelings of both abandonment and betrayal as they attempt to move out into the world. Their co-dependence pulls them into continued involvement in the family because it seems necessary for emotional survival. At the same time, their natural impulse to mature tells them that separation is necessary for emotional growth, and ultimately for spiritual survival. Frequently, in therapy ACoAs begin to remember solemn promises made to themselves during childhood, which later interfere with their efforts to detach from their families. In particular, the promise not to abandon those who need them confuses their normal desire to enter into full and independent adulthood. As long as the family continues to suffer from alcoholism, the ACoA feels guilty of callously abandoning them by the simple act of moving away from home, much as they felt abandoned as a youngster. As we shall see shortly, such promises were made from a co-dependent perspective. It is not that the promise must be broken, but rather the co-dependent perspective must be relinquished.

=11=

Co-dependence As A Normal Childhood Reaction To Stress

I n the second chapter I said that feeling pain is not the goal of resurrecting the past. In this chapter I want to say that it was not the pain during your childhood that wounded you as much as it was the ways you discovered, and were taught, to avoid that pain. Our defenses can become the problem in the same way that our immune system can become hyperactive and create dangerous allergies or asthma.

Children naturally become co-dependent when raised in tense and chaotic circumstances. Your own survival instincts led you to a distorted view of your responsibilities. Unfortunately, your family intensified these distortions by treating co-dependence as normal adult behavior.

Reasons For Developing The Co-dependent View

As youngsters, we develop a co-dependent view of the world for the following reasons. Our evolutionary heritage provides us with the biological and psychological tools for getting adults to bond tightly to us. Babies are particularly satisfying to suckle and to hold. They elicit frequent contact with their parents, unless their parents are intoxicated and insensitive to the intimacy the infant needs and, in turn, can provide. When children's efforts to connect with those who are responsible for their safety and care encounter alcoholic/co-dependent parents, the results are confusing, and provoke intense anxiety. One moment the bond feels real; the next moment it is gone. At another time the bond is present but consists primarily of anger. Often, the family will treat the bond as real, even though the parents' thoughts and feelings are not truly present.

As children look out at the world of adults, they see giants and gods who literally have the power of life and death over them. A realistic assessment of the capricious, arbitrary behavior that such giants demonstrate when intoxicated would be overwhelming to a child. It creates such anxiety and hopelessness that further development becomes difficult.

On the other hand, one small distortion on a child's part has the power to rescue hope and keep it alive. Built into our developing minds is the omnipotent attitude that we are the primary cause of all the things that happen to us. If our parents treat us inconsistently, or abandon or mistreat us, we tend to see ourselves as causing their behavior. In effect, children of alcoholics have a choice of seeing themselves either as saints in a world of sinners or as sinners in a world of saints. If the stark reality of being at the mercy of a dangerous world were clearly understood, children would have little hope of eventually gaining control of their lives.

Those who accept the delusion that they are causing their parents' erratic behavior are left with the belief that they can eventually attain safety. They work hard to improve them- selves, in hopes of no longer causing their parent's drinking behavior. The hope is that they can live in Eden, if they can only grow up far enough; so they strive forever to eliminate their "badness."

If basic trust is not well-developed, hope becomes an acceptable alternative. However, if both trust and hope are missing, a child is far more likely to become a casualty.

Relinquishing The Co-dependent View

The paradox for ACoAs is that the co-dependent illusion of causing their parents' alcoholism and being responsible for the resulting emotional/physical abandonment is useful during childhood, but it becomes a burden to them as adults. As a child, co-dependence helps safeguard the normal impulse to mature. However, to enter into full adulthood, the co-dependent stance must eventually be relinquished. The realities of childhood, at last, must be acknowledged. The process of dismantling this co-dependent illusion of omnipotence is called recovery. Chapters 13-17 focus on what recovery means.

=12=

Recognizing Emotional Abuse

When children's development of self-esteem, social skills or capacity for intimacy is jeopardized by their parents' behavior or neglect, they may be the victim of emotional abuse. It is here that the experience of ACoAs and adults from other dysfunctional families overlaps the most. Whether it is alcohol or other drugs, mental illness, compulsive behavior (eating, working, religiosity, etc.), or any one of a thousand other things that deplete a family's emotional life, the results are the same. Children are left to their own devices to make sense of the pain and loneliness in their life.

In a book called *The Psychologically Battered Child* (Garbarino, et al., Jossey-Bass Publishers, 1985), emotional abuse is identified as a *pattern* of "rejecting, isolating, terrorizing, ignoring and corrupting" behavior on the part of one's parent. What do each of these words mean?

The Elements Of Emotional Abuse

Rejecting Behavior

Rejecting behavior means that the adults in your life refuse (or are unable) to acknowledge your worth or the legitimacy of your needs. Rejecting frequently happens, both directly and subtly, in alcoholic families. Alcoholics are usually locked in a battle with their own sense of worthlessness, and the co-dependents are unconvinced that their own needs are legitimate. When adults are imprisoned by their own *self*-rejection, they are unable to instill a sense of worth in their children. You can not give away what you do not have. At the worst, out of control parents can systematically attack their children's self-esteem, mocking their needs and openly competing with them.

Isolating Behavior

Isolating behavior means that adults prevent their child from having normal social contacts or forming friendships. The result is that their children begin believing they are alone in this world. Children of alcoholics feel that their experience is unique — that no one could possibly understand them. Sometimes it is the shame of allowing friends see your drunk parent which keeps CoAs from inviting friends over to their home. Other times parents actively keep their children from participating in normal childhood activities, as they fall into their own isolation from the world to hide their drinking. In one way or another, alcoholics' sense of being separate and misunderstood is communicated to their children, who do not have the tools to deal with such loneliness.

Terrorizing Behavior

Terrorizing behavior means that adults may verbally assault and bully children, and create a climate of fear that leads their children to believe that the world is a capricious and hostile place. There may be nothing more profoundly disturbing than to see your own parent be out of control. Parents are supposed to provide the consistency, the maturity and the self-discipline to help children develop their own self-control. This is impossible when one or both parents are alcoholic and mired in their own daily battle with losing control. Once intoxicated, many adults lose all civility. Their anger spews forth like venom. And home becomes a terrifying place to be.

Ignoring Behavior

Ignoring behavior means that adults no longer stimulate or respond to their children. The connection with parents is lost, as they become emotionally unreachable. Alcoholics may become absent by passing out. They may also become absent by retreating into their own worlds of intoxication. Most young children are not capable of recognizing that their parents' unresponsiveness is the result of their drinking. As a result, kids are frequently left wondering what they have done to cause their parents to ignore them. Even when not intoxicated, alcoholic parents can be very self-centered, as long as their disease remains untreated. This self-absorption is one symptom of alcoholism and contributes further to children's sense of having lost the essential connection they need to their parent.

Corrupting Behavior

Corrupting behavior means that adults serve as negative role models for their children or actually stimulate their children to engage in destructive behavior. Most people would agree that alcoholic drinking is a poor lifestyle to teach your children, even if the teaching is only by example. The sadder case is when children are encouraged to join the drinking when they are still quite young. For many ACoAs, their only way to feel a part of their family, even when they were in grade school, was to get drunk with everyone else. Another form of corrupting behavior may come from the co-

dependent parents' encouragement to excuse the drinking
or to suppress whatever negative feelings their children
might have. Although this initiation into a co-dependent
lifestyle does not put children at odds with social norms, it
does put them at odds with their true selves. And we have
already looked at the price paid for this.

The Effects Of Emotional Abuse

The effects of emotional abuse are varied, partly depend-
ing on what age the abuse was suffered, what other negative
factors may be present (physical abuse, sexual abuse, family
disintegration, etc.) and what other mitigating factors may be
present (especially a healthy surrogate parent). In general,
however, emotionally abused children tend to be anxious,
and to feel unloved and unlovable, inferior, angry and
defective. It is common to see them cling to a parent and, yet,
move away when their parent tries to get closer. They are
wary. They have been burned.

These are the ways that ACoAs and adults from other
dysfunctional homes are alike. The process of recovering
from these wounds is also the same, and it is time to focus
attention on solutions to the problems we have been
outlining.

13

The Recovery Process

When alcoholics stop drinking, they are often faced with the unwelcome fact that their abstinence is only the first of many difficult changes that must be made. Many alcoholics refuse to attempt changes beyond abstinence and, as a result, do not enter into the recovery process. They are captured by the delusion that a full and rich life will result merely from not drinking. But simply avoiding alcohol has the same effect on the mind as telling yourself that your nose does not itch. Actually, concentrating on not drinking intensifies the devotion to control and willpower. Sobriety is an active process, motivated by an attraction to the riches of a full emotional life. It can never be attained merely by the elimination of drinking.

Awareness

What do alcoholics and co-dependents need to do to enter into recovery? They need to increase their awareness at critical times when they feel threatened, defensive or closed. We can restrict our awareness in more ways than one can imagine. Drinking restricts our awareness, but that is only one way. We can also ignore our feelings, force ourselves to forget whatever is unpleasant, daydream, intellectualize, defend, deny, not pay attention, phase out, go to sleep, avoid conflicts, get depressed, have a panic attack and on and on. When alcoholics give up drinking but continue to make use of all the other ways of remaining unaware, they have not made the fundamental change that leads to an authentic recovery. Instead, they are as fully involved in using willpower to manage all aspects of their lives as ever. When their energy is nearly exhausted by these purely psychological means, the occasional use of alcohol provides an alternate means that is still consistent with their basic approach to life, that is, "What you don't know can't hurt you."

Co-dependent Issues

Alcoholics enter into full recovery only when they begin to face their co-dependent issues, as well as their addiction to alcohol. A remarkable number of alcoholics find it impossible to take an honest look at their co-dependence until the desperate crises created by their drinking motivate them. Nonalcoholic co-dependents frequently have even more difficulty seeing the need for their own recovery. Their co-dependent perspective is too comfortable because they can blame their misery and low self-esteem on the alcoholic. The truth is that recovery from co-dependence is often a matter of life and death for both the alcoholic and the nonalcoholic, and the steps toward recovery for both are identical. Co-dependence is co-dependence, whether alcoholism is superimposed on it or not. Recovery from co-dependence requires an active search for the denial in one's life and a commitment to dismantle that denial, regardless of the realities that will be uncovered.

Although recovery is an active process, it also involves the discipline of letting go. This can best be illustrated by imagining two men wading out in the ocean. When a mammoth wave unexpectedly breaks over them, two reactions are possible. The unrecovering co-dependent digs his heels into the sand, stiffens his body and attempts to counter the wave's overwhelming power. The recovering co-dependent recognizes the futility of resisting such a great force and reacts by going with the force of the wave. When the time is right, and much of the wave's power is spent, this individual will have the energy left to swim toward the surface. The "letting go" of recovery leaves you with all your energy still available for dealing with life realistically. The unrecovering approach expends much of its energy before any effective action could possibly be taken. The meaning of the above illustration is best expressed in the traditional "Serenity Prayer":

> God, grant me the serenity
> To accept the things I cannot change,
> Courage to change the things I can,
> And the wisdom to know the difference.

Before recovery, we are obsessed with trying to prove we can change things that ultimately lie beyond our power to change. As recovery progresses, we pay more attention to being effective and less to being powerful.

The recovery process takes place in a series of stages. These stages are discussed in the next chapter.

═14═

Stages Of Recovery

R ecovery occurs in predictable stages. These stages are
the same whether or not a co-dependent is also
alcoholic. A major source of healing for ACoAs is to
recognize that their own recovery essentially
involves the same task faced by their parents. There
is far more that ACoAs and their alcoholic parents have in
common than separates them. As they experience difficulties
with their own recovery, ACoAs will come to feel empathy for
the illness affecting their parents.

Five Stages In The Recovery Process

There are five stages in the recovery process.* These
include: the Survivor Stage, the Identification Stage, the Core
Issues Stage, the Integration Stage and Genesis.

The Survivor Stage

Many alcoholics are caught in this stage of recovery. They need to drink to avoid feeling sicker than they already feel. Seizures, DTs and intense self-recrimination are the experiences they risk facing if they stop drinking. Drinking provides a greater feeling of well-being and normalcy than does early abstinence. Consequently, denial feels necessary for sheer survival.

ACoAs who deny that their parents are alcoholic or refuse to look at how they really feel about their parents' drinking, are in the survivor stage. Anger and sadness are held in tightly in order to avoid becoming overwhelmed by the awareness of their parents' alcoholism. The reins on one's spontaneity are held taut in a constant effort to feel and appear normal. Again, denial seems necessary for sheer survival.

Although the survivor stage is the first stage of the recovery process, recovery does not actually begin until the identification stage.

The Identification Stage

For alcoholics, this stage begins the moment they shift from a refusal to acknowledge that they are alcoholic, to a more realistic acceptance of their disease. Two things are particularly important about the act of shifting one's identity from that of a nonalcoholic to that of an alcoholic. First, the change involves taking a great leap by faith alone. Alcoholics must "let go" of denial as their means of survival. This is done without any guarantee that anything will get better once they have acknowledged their alcoholism. Second, simply identifying oneself as an alcoholic will not initiate the recovery process. It can only do so when it also involves a realization that one's relationship to willpower has been grossly distorted. Mouthing the words that you are an alcoholic is wasted energy. In order to be meaningful, these words must also be accompanied by a shift in the boundaries of one's very self-image. During the identification stage, the alcoholic's self-image shrinks from the overblown, controlling state in the survival stage to more realistic dimensions.

This shrinkage is often a profound and spiritual experience. Anytime that we experience a more realistic relationship between ourselves and the universe, our spirit is energized. At the same time, it can also be frightening and deflating.

ACoAs must begin their own recovery with a similar shift in their self-image. The identification stage involves a more realistic assessment of the past, and must include a new awareness of one's true relationship to willpower. Many ACoAs get stuck half way through this stage, as do many alcoholics. Acknowledging that you are an adult child of an alcoholic provides a framework upon which you can construct a realistic view of the past for the first time. An outpouring of feelings can occur once ACoAs drop their denial and see the events of their family's past in a more realistic light. Anger, which has long been stifled or redirected toward themselves, is at last directed outward. However, unless this is balanced by an honest evaluation of one's own continuing co-dependent distortions, full recovery is not possible. For both the alcoholic and the ACoA, the identification stage is not complete until a full acknowledgment of their distorted relationship to control issues is made.

There is a subtle, but critical, difference between acknowledging that you have an alcoholic parent and understanding that *you* are the child of an alcoholic. The first view keeps the focus outside of yourself and in the past. This is a valuable beginning and can pave the way for important changes, but it does not go far enough in and of itself. The second view puts the focus back on yourself and in the present. It is in the present that your relationship with willpower may be continuing to create problems. And it is in the present that this relationship has to be revised.

AA embodies what has been said earlier about the admission of powerlessness made in the first of its Twelve Steps of recovery. If individuals are unwilling to see that their power is limited, they are not ready for recovery. Their co-dependent delusions are still too strong. It should come as no surprise that Al-Anon, the self-help group for families of alcoholics, has adopted the same steps for its own recovery program.

Following the identification stage, recovering ACoAs move on to the core issues stage.

The Core Issues Stage

This stage involves an active exploration of the ways that our refusal to admit powerlessness and our fear of being out of control are affecting our lives. It is a time for both the alcoholic and the ACoA to recognize their co-dependence. Examples of co-dependence control issues include the following:

1. Difficulty knowing feelings and trusting others enough to express these feelings honestly
2. Lacking spontaneity
3. Needing to maintain a protective facade
4. Denying either emotional or physical needs
5. Basing self-esteem on how others see you

Recovery is a continuous process of acknowledging the more realistic limits to willpower and thereby letting go of cherished delusions. Gradually, the areas of effectiveness in your life increase as less and less energy is wasted on trying to change things beyond your control. As you give up trying to dictate which feelings you will and will not allow yourself, you find your emotional life awakening, stretching painfully and beginning to ebb and flow with a life of its own.

The recovery process continues to the integration stage, where new belief systems are integrated.

The Integration Stage

By this stage, the recovery process is nearly identical, whether your primary identity is that of an ACoA, a co-dependent or an alcoholic. Everyone is faced with the task of developing belief systems that legitimize self-acceptance. During the Integration Stage, transformations of core attitudes begin to be woven together into a new fabric for your life. The wounds have been acknowledged and grieved for now, permitting you to begin focusing on the strengths within yourself that have survived. Characteristics that have been liabilities become assets. For example, the extreme sensitivity to others' feelings can be used to great advantage by those ACoAs in the helping professions. During the integration stage, maintaining personal integrity becomes more important than managing our life in a way that we imagine will make us happy. In other words, rather than trying to control our feelings or other people, we are able to state our needs and emotions clearly, allowing others to react to them as they wish. A basic faith in honesty, for its own sake, becomes a part of daily life.

During the Integration Stage, a Personal Bill of Rights is developed. It includes items such as**:

1. Life should have choices beyond mere survival.
2. You have a right to say no to anything when you feel you are not ready, or it's unsafe.
3. Life should not be motivated by fear.
4. You have a right to all of your feelings.
5. You are probably not guilty.
6. You have a right to make mistakes.
7. There is no need to smile when you cry.
8. You have a right to terminate conversations with people who make you feel put down and humiliated.
9. You can be healthier than those around you.
10. It is okay to be relaxed, playful and frivolous.
11. You have a right to change and grow.
12. It is important to set limits and to be selfish.
13. You can be angry at someone you love.
14. You can take care of yourself, no matter what your circumstances are.

Genesis

The final stage of recovery is called Genesis. This stage will be different for each person. Up to this point, recovery has been a process of becoming actors, rather than reactors. In Genesis, we begin participating in the creation of our own world. The life we produce for ourselves is an accurate expression of the life that moves within us. Genesis is the true beginning.

The five stages of recovery described here illustrate the steps involved in the recovery process. Besides understanding the stages of recovery, it is important to know there are various aids to help you through the process.

---

*I am especially indebted to Herbert Gravitz and Julie Bowden, whose description of the stages of recovery is presented at much greater length in *Recovery: A Guide For Children Of Alcoholics* (Simon & Schuster, 1987).

**Items on this list stem from Claudia Black, Herbert Gravitz, Julie Bowden and Jael Greenleaf.

═══ 15 ═══

Tools For Recovery

Tools to help you through the recovery process can include: a self-help program guided by the Twelve Steps, such as Al-Anon and the newer ACA Fellowship; therapy, both individual and group; and an increasing variety of literature on the subject.

Twelve-Step Programs

Every ACoA's recovery should include at least an investigation of the various Twelve-Step programs available today. The Twelve Steps, which proved so valuable as the backbone of Alcoholics Anonymous, have also been valuable to nonalcoholic co-dependents. During the 1940s family members of alcoholics began applying the Twelve Steps to their own lives and created Al-Anon Family Groups (1951). Six years later

Al-Anon began the first groups for teenage children of alcoholics, called Alateen.

During the 1980s, meetings with a special focus on adult children of alcoholics appeared and spread like wildfire across the country. Today, Al-Anon has registered over 1,000 weekly meetings and estimates that an equal number of unregistered meetings exist. In addition, an entirely separate organization named the ACA Fellowship has emerged and has a number of meetings similar to Al-Anon's. Both of these programs continue to grow rapidly, as more and more adult children of alcoholics seek out Twelve-Step fellowships as part of their recovery.

Whether the Twelve Steps make sense to you at first or not, it is usually beneficial to ponder the many levels of meaning contained in each. Many recovering people find that understanding the Steps gradually deepens as they meditate quietly on them. Even if the Steps never prove useful, it is often a valuable experience to sit in a room with other ACoAs, all of whom are working toward a more honest appraisal of their lives. For many ACoAs, as for many alcoholics, the Twelve-Step program is likely to be a life-long tool for recovery.

The differences between Al-Anon adult children of alcoholics and ACA meetings are minimal when each has a healthy regard for concentrating on working the Twelve Steps. The best advice is to try a few meetings in each fellowship and to look for meetings that stick closely to the original, successful format developed by AA. Such meetings take the Twelve Steps and Traditions seriously. Once you become familiar with these guidelines, it is easy to determine whether a particular meeting is right for you.

Therapy

How does seeing a therapist differ from talking to a good friend? At times, there may be little difference. Both a friend and a therapist may listen with empathy to your feelings. Both may help you see new ways of solving problems that you have been overlooking. Both can lend important support when you begin to make difficult changes in your life.

But there are other times when the difference between a therapist and a friend can be enormous. Therapists are trained to keep their own bias out of the work they do with you. The entire purpose of the relationship is that *your* own needs and goals get met. It is not healthy for a friend to relate to you in such a one-sided manner for very long. Furthermore, therapists are trained to understand the subtleties of how festering childhood wounds disrupt current relationships, including the very relationship that develops between yourself and the therapist. Finally, therapists not only understand how problems develop, but they also have perspective on the entire healing process. They know how to use the relationship with you to stimulate your own ability to heal yourself. Then, after setting this healing in motion, good therapists do not foster dependency on themselves, but rather have the willingness to let you separate from them and lead your own life.

In some ways, a good therapist can become a stand-in for your parent and can allow the child within you to complete much of the business that was buried alive when you were young. This is too much to ask of a friend. It demands special skills. And it is best to separate when your work is done. You may need to come back again at some point in the future and finish another layer of work. Let your therapist remain a therapist. And let your friends remain friends.

Gradually, therapy is becoming available for ACoAs, but the field is still so new that there are no agreed on standards for the training experiences that properly prepare a therapist to deal effectively with ACoA issues. Many well-meaning therapists have recognized the need for services to ACoAs and have rushed in to provide help. But, high percentages of these therapists are ACoAs themselves, many of whom have never looked at their own issues and may have important blind spots.

Anyone seeking therapy needs to be aware that not all therapists are equally skilled, particularly in the new field of ACoA issues. Good intentions do not automatically translate into good therapy. In choosing a therapist, I suggest you pay attention to the following points:

1. Does the therapist have training or experience in alcoholism?
2. Does the therapist have a good background in child development?
3. Has the therapist had specific training in co-dependence?
4. If an ACoA, has the therapist received treatment for co-dependence?

Professionals who are untreated ACoAs can be recognized by the way they:

1. Encourage your anger for their own purposes
2. Intellectualize, rather than encourage the expression of emotion
3. Easily become defensive
4. Are uncomfortable with silence
5. Resist exploring Twelve-Step programs
6. Push you into action before you are ready
7. Are certain that they have already dealt with all of their co-dependence issues

The question of whether therapists must be ACoAs themselves has no easy answer. Sometimes people are comforted by the fact that their therapist has had firsthand experience with an alcoholic parent. This builds trust quickly. Other times people are comforted by knowing that their therapist has a more objective viewpoint or, at least, that their blind spots will not match. Both ACoAs and non-ACoAs can make good therapists. It is more important that the therapists you choose are competent than that they are also ACoAs.

Perhaps the first question to be answered regarding therapy is whether to enter individual therapy or group therapy. Both can be valuable, but the focus is different for each. Individual therapy has the advantage of intense exploration of your own particular issues, including your relationship to authority figures. It may also be useful for people whose feelings tend to freeze in group situations. Individual therapy has the disadvantage of giving ACoAs only one person to whom they have to be sensitive, making it easier for them to maintain their facade. Also, it does not provide the validation they might receive from other ACoAs in a group situation. Such validation can become a constant source of healing.

Group Therapy

Group therapy has the advantage of symbolically re-creating the family environment for ACoAs, which quickly activates important control issues and makes them available for exploration. The direct interaction with other ACoAs is an invaluable part of the therapeutic process of group therapy. The major disadvantages are the unavailability of groups organized for the specific purpose of dealing with ACoA issues, and the tendency of therapists to run time-limited groups or to be overly active in guiding the group. The skill required to do group therapy is frequently underestimated.

Group therapy is conducted at several different depths and intensities.

Education Groups

Education groups are designed to impart factual information and stimulate recognition of attitudes and feelings that have previously remained hidden.

Time-Limited Groups

Time-limited groups usually last six to ten weeks and are designed to help ACoAs further explore relevant issues. They include time-limited support groups and experiential groups. Time-limited support groups are designed to lead partici-pants through discussions of major issues, with each meeting organized around specific topics, such as fear of feelings, trust, expressing needs, etc. Time-limited experiential groups place emphasis on exercises that are specifically designed to activate a person's feelings. Such groups can be powerful, and are especially effective if the participants also have a place to develop a framework for understanding their feelings and systematically working toward changing their behavior.

Long-Term Interactional Groups

These groups last long enough that members can no longer hold back from each other and use the excuse that the group just started, *or* that it is about to end. In this type of group therapy, the therapists are much less directive. By commenting on the patterns of interaction observed among group members, therapists are able to help participants see how they re-create situations in the group that illustrate their difficulties with relationships. This kind of interaction provides the group members an opportunity to discover which roles they play and how those roles determine the kind of world in which they live. Long-term interactional groups for ACoAs distill and intensify co-dependent behaviors, while simultaneously providing a supportive atmosphere for experimenting with new behaviors.

Individual Therapy

Individual therapy varies so widely that no useful generalizations can be made. Each technique depends largely on the personal qualities of the therapist for its effectiveness. I tend to conduct individual therapy simultaneously on two parallel tracks, one dealing with PTSD symptoms and the other with co-dependent symptoms. The theoretical basis for choosing this method is that the symptoms from both of these conditions each require somewhat different approaches to their treatment.

Post-Traumatic Stress Disorder leaves people fearful of being overwhelmed by feelings. Simply pushing ACoAs into expressing themselves emotionally can greatly intensify this fear and justify their rigid emotional control. Therapy should help people develop freedom to experience their feelings, as well as freedom to put the brakes on their feelings when necessary. Once people gain confidence in their ability to move back and forth between opening up or closing down, they then have the confidence they need to explore their emotions fully. I work by helping ACoAs identify concrete body sensations associated with each feeling. Visualization techniques are used to help them take full measure of these feelings. They are always encouraged to take responsibility for backing away from, as well as entering into, feeling states. While they are experiencing moments of intense feelings, I ask them to report on how old they feel and then to free associate about their life at that age. In this way, a more realistic picture of their childhood feelings is gradually exposed. These feelings are explored until the effect of alcoholism on the family is understood, including the coping style they adopted as a result.

Co-dependent symptoms are dealt with by carefully exploring an ACoA's current relationship with themselves, their parents, the rest of their family, work, play, chemical substances and ultimately with me, as their therapist. When the opportunity arises, parallels in coping styles between the past and the present are identified. ACoAs are then faced with the question of whether or not behavior required in the past for survival is still helpful. If not, opportunities to change current behavior are further explored.

Conferences And Workshops

A wide variety of conferences and workshops are becoming available for ACoAs. Getting on the mailing list for your state chapter of the National Association for Children of Alcoholics (NACoA) or your local National Council on Alcoholism (NCA) should help you keep aware of what is happening in your area. These forums are an excellent source of information and frequently provide a safe place for new or more intense feelings to surface.

It is also best to be aware that conferences and workshops are not therapy. They can never substitute for the long, often hard work that must go into recovery. What they *can* do is open up new perspectives for you, educate you and bring you into closer contact with the recovering ACoA community. At times, the intense experience of workshops can also open issues that are best handled in therapy.

Literature

A growing body of useful literature is becoming available for ACoAs. However, these books and pamphlets should never be taken too seriously. Different authors have different views. Many of these views may be helpful, but few are the truth. Use them like kernels of grain in a grist mill. Throw them in, grind them up and make your own bread from the flour they provide.

Also be aware that recovery never comes out of a book. It comes out of you. Don't measure the depth of your recovery by the height of ACoA books you have piled on your shelf. If books draw you out and into the company of others who are recovering, they have served a useful purpose. If they become one more screen to hide your face behind, one more way you isolate yourself from others or one more source of intellectual concepts to protect yourself from your feelings, they are not serving you well.

A list of helpful literature can be found at the end of this book.

═══ 16 ═══

Putting The Discipline Of Recovery Into Action

N ow that you know all this about being an ACoA, why don't you feel any better?

The answer to this question is simple, and it is difficult at the same time. The simple part has to do with the fact that recovery is far more than knowledge, just as raising a crop requires far more than a bag of seeds you hold in your hand in the spring. The difficult part of the answer is that recovery requires the kind of discipline based on faith, not on willpower.

Discipline, time and patience are needed. Just as the farmer must prepare the soil, plant the seeds, water, weed, hope for the right weather and wait for the miracle of new life to lift its head up from the earth and stretch its leaves toward the sky, so must each of us nurture our recovery and wait for the harvest to come in its own time. You cannot command or control it any more than the farmer can force the weather to behave or order a plant to grow faster than is its nature.

Awareness And Actions

Healing comes through a balance between *awareness* and *action*. It cannot be forced any more than we can force water to flow away from the sea. We *can* deepen the existing river bed and sometimes straighten it a bit, allowing the water to flow more freely. But it is useless to try to make water flow uphill. Like water, healing flows through channels that are etched in our minds and hearts. Our efforts to encourage healing must move through these natural channels and avoid forcing growth along paths that do not exist.

Honesty, Feelings And Community

Just as the body heals cuts if we keep the wound clean, there are actions we can take to nurture the forces that heal our heart. We can practice rigid honesty. We can willingly invite our feelings into our lives. And we can commit ourselves to enter fully into community with others. When consistently practiced, each of these actions moves us beyond mere awareness, and into a new and healthier life.

Rigid honesty cleanses the mind of the distortions that denial creates. I believe that real healing does not begin until your mind is focused on the *realities* affecting your life, and is no longer filled with illusions or left vacant by lost memories. You cannot expect real healing to occur while you remain identified with your false self or before you are aware of the actual wounds you have suffered.

Making room in your life for feelings revitalizes the mind, the heart and the soul. A willingness to experience your emotions means touching each facet of them and taking the full measure of their depth. When you invite your feelings into your presence like you would receive an honored and welcome guest into your home, then they can move freely through your life without draining your energies.

I believe that the mind heals only if our feelings are experienced instead of just dealt with intellectually. Feelings are alive; they are not simply ideas. They breathe, stretch, squirm and need rest. The more we try to control and disavow them, the more they turn around and control us. Emotions behave differently when confined in a cage instead of being able to move freely. When your willpower imposes a master-servant relationship on your feelings, no one wins. A willingness to experience your feelings creates a partnership with them. This partnership permits the natural healing forces of the mind to be effective.

Joining the community of recovering ACoAs greatly speeds the mind's healing. By trusting others enough to let them see who you really are, a new sense of belonging begins. I believe that seeing yourself as part of a larger whole is invariably healing. Community adds dimension and purpose to your life that can never be generated wholly from within. We are too small to create what community alone brings into our lives. We can never break out of our isolation on our own.

Honesty, feelings and community are the actions you can take each day to nurture your healing. Whether these actions pay off in the moment or not, a program of recovery calls on us to practice them as an act of faith. The awareness that they bring may often be uncomfortable. But they are releasing the natural forces of healing, nonetheless. Discipline, time and patience allow your healing to happen at its maximum speed.

If this is too slow for your taste, talk about these feelings honestly with those you can trust. But do not fall back into the delusion that you can hurry things up by force of will. That strategy is bankrupt. Instead, practice honesty, feelings and community each day. The bounty they eventually bring will be beyond your wildest dreams.

=17=

National Association For Children Of Alcoholics (NACoA)

ar too many children of alcoholics reach adulthood without ever receiving the support and education they need to cope effectively with their parents' alcoholism. In 1983, a nonprofit organization named the National Association for Children of Alcoholics (NACoA) was founded to end the silence that permits this to happen.

Goal

The goal of NACoA is to create a powerful voice, promoting awareness of CoA issues among children of alcoholics themselves, throughout the alcoholism and mental health fields, and in the public at large. With 20 state chapters already established, NACoA is dedicated to ending the silence that has surrounded alcoholic families, once and for all.

Membership

The NACoA provides an opportunity for adult children of alcoholics to continue their own recovery by participating in the solution and helping to ensure that today's young CoAs are given the information they need, when they need it. By joining NACoA, you can reach across generations to your younger brothers and sisters, and touch on the child within yourself as well.

We are a membership organization, and your yearly dues support important work, such as the Elementary School Project, which sent a packet of information to the more than 47,000 public elementary schools in America. The packet included a guidebook for teachers to help them identify CoAs in the classroom, six full color posters picturing Marvel Comics figures, such as Spiderman and Captain America speaking directly to kids with "Moms and Dads who drink too much," and a comic book on emotional abuse developed by the National Committee for the Prevention of Child Abuse. Membership is a donation and a commitment to the future. Its reward is the gratification that comes with knowing that you are contributing to changing the world for millions of youngsters.

As ACoAs, we share a common bond. We always have. The NACoA is dedicated to changing the code of silence and secrecy that has been our bond for so long, to a bond that comes from reaching out together to share our healing with those who are still waiting for help.

I invite you to become a member of NACoA and to make a contribution to continue its important work. Write to:

NACoA
31582 Coast Highway, Suite B
South Laguna, CA 92677-3044
(714) 499-3889

Afterword

Now that I have completed the writing of this booklet for adult children of alcoholics, I feel good. Many of the ideas presented here have been rumbling through my mind for some time. Most have been part of lectures I have given, and attended at various workshops and conferences. Putting them all together in one place has given me a nice sense of completion. Now the hard part begins.

By the hard part, I mean letting the booklet go; putting it out for ACoAs to use. It is time to stop worrying about what it could have been and let it be what it is. I pray that it will offer more guidance than confusion, more hope than fear and real healing for those who find it in their hands.

I want to close with a story. The story is an actual occurrence from a long-term interactive group I have been privileged to co-lead for over a year. Janice, a member of the group, struggled with a deep sadness she felt within. If she fully assumed the label of an adult child of an alcoholic, she would have to allow herself to feel the intensity of what that meant to her. However, she feared that the full intensity of her sadness would be too much to tolerate. She described feeling as though she were on the brink of a bottomless black pit, with her sanity lying somewhere on the other shore.

Janice was indecisive about committing herself to experiencing the sadness. She knew she could not be happy staying where she was in her denial, but there were no guarantees that she would ever emerge again if she experienced the depth of her sadness. Finally, she relied on the basic lessons she learned from her own recovery from alcoholism. She let go of trying to determine how things were going to work out ahead of time and took a leap of faith. For the next ten minutes, Janice felt wave after wave of sadness overcome her. The rest of the group sat silently as her tears slowly came to the surface. Then she sobbed uncontrollably, and without shame. Eventually, the sadness seemed to ease, and the crying tapered away. When she felt ready, Janice opened her eyes and told the group what she had just experienced.

"I was right," she said. "The sadness is bottomless. When I dove in, it was like being swallowed by a pool of heavy darkness. I just kept sinking. But I didn't fight it, so that the crying just got deeper and deeper as I got more lost in the sadness . . . God, it hurts.

"But then I began to feel something like warm air bubbles coming up around me. I actually felt them all over my body. They began to buoy me upwards. It was like I was rising toward the surface of the pool without having to make any effort myself. When I broke through the surface, I knew for the first time that it no longer matters whether my sadness is bottomless or not. It has a surface, and I will not get lost in the darkness."

She sat back and looked at the circle of the group members around her. Then Janice looked surprised and added, "I was lifted out of my sadness by your support and caring."

She swept her arms out to point to the circle of people in the group and to show how it felt like their concern was wrapped around her as protection. "I was always afraid to let my feelings be seen by other people," she said. "But, if I had tried to do what I just did when I was alone, I don't know what would have happened. The support this group gives me is a real life preserver."

Janice's story illustrates how, together, we can come to experience the fullness and richness of our lives. Together we can come to understand the past for what it really was and acknowledge the truth about how we feel about the past. Together we can recover more fully than we can alone.

Suggested Reading

The following books will help you explore further what it means to be the child of an alcoholic:

General

Black, Claudia. **It Will Never Happen To Me.** Denver, CO: Medical Administration, 1982.

Bowden, Julie, and Gravitz, Herbert. **Genesis: Spirituality In Recovery From Childhood Traumas.** Pompano Beach, FL: Health Communications, 1988.

Brooks, Cathleen. **The Secret Everyone Knows.** San Diego, CA: The Kroc Foundation, 1981.

Cermak, Timmen. **A Time To Heal.** Los Angeles, CA: Jeremy Tarcher, 1988.

Cermak, Timmen. **Diagnosing And Treating Co-dependence.** Minneapolis, MN: Johnson Institute Books, 1986.

Gravitz, Herbert, and Bowden, Julie. **Guide To Recovery: A Book For Adult Children Of Alcoholics.** New York, NY: Simon & Schuster, 1987.

Gravitz, Herbert. **Children Of Alcoholics Handbook**. South Laguna, CA: The National Association for Children of Alcoholics, 1985.

Leite, E., and Espeland, P. **Different Like Me: A Book For Teens Who Worry About Their Parents' Use Of Alcohol/Drugs**. Minneapolis, MN: Johnson Institute Books, 1987.

Lerner, Rokelle. **Daily Affirmations**. Pompano Beach, FL: Health Communications, 1985.

O'Gorman, Patricia, and Oliver-Diaz, Philip. **Breaking The Cycle Of Addiction: A Parent's Guide To Raising Healthy Kids**. Pompano Beach, FL: Health Communications, 1987.

Subby, Robert. **Lost In The Shuffle: The Co-dependent Reality**. Pompano Beach, FL: Health Communications, 1987.

Wegscheider, Sharon. **Another Chance: Hope And Health For The Alcoholic Family**. Palo Alto, CA: Science & Behavior Books, 1981.

Wholey, Dennis. **Becoming Your Own Parent**. New York, NY: Doubleday, 1988.

Woititz, Janet. **Adult Children Of Alcoholics**. Pompano Beach, FL: Health Communications, 1983.

Biography

Scales, Cynthia. **Potato Chips For Breakfast**. Rockaway, NJ: Quotidian Press, 1986.

Somers, Suzanne. **Keeping Secrets**. New York, NY: Warner Books, 1988.

Twelve-Step Recovery

Julia H. **Letting Go With Love: Help For Those Who Love An Alcoholic/Addict**. Los Angeles, CA: Jeremy Tarcher, 1987.

Rachel V. **Family Secrets: Life Stories Of Adult Children Of Alcoholics**. New York, NY: Harper & Row, 1987.

The **Twelve Steps For Adult Children.** San Diego, CA: Recovery Publications, 1987.

The **Twelve Steps: A Way Out — A Working Guide For Adult Children Of Alcoholics And Other Families.** San Diego, CA: Recovery Publications, 1987.

Workbooks

Black, Claudia. **Repeat After Me: Workbook For Adult Children.** Denver, CO: Medical Administration, 1985.

McConnell, Patty. **Adult Children Of Alcoholics: A Workbook For Healing.** New York, NY: Harper & Row, 1986.

Alcoholism

Johnson, Vernon E. **I'll Quit Tomorrow.** New York, NY: Harper & Row, 1973. (Available through Johnson Institute, 510 First Avenue North, Minneapolis, MN 55403.)

Johnson, Vernon E. **Intervention: How To Help Someone Who Doesn't Want Help.** Minneapolis, MN: Johnson Institute Books, 1986.

Milam, James R., and Ketcham, Katherine. **Under The Influence.** New York, NY: Bantam Books, 1983.

Bibliography

Ackerman, Robert J. **Children Of Alcoholics: Bibliography And Resource Guide.** 3rd ed. Deerfield Beach, FL: Health Communications, 1987.